DANGER, GOD WORKING OVERHEAD

God putting the cat out . . .

Danger, God Working Overhead

CAROLINE HOLDEN

Methuen

for Harry

Also by Caroline Holden

Securi Skunk

Books illustrated by Caroline Holden

The Lion and Albert, Albert Comes Back (*Marriott Edgar*)

Fishy Business, Microfish, Nervous Wreck (*Robert Lee*)

Small Harry and the Toothache Pills (*Michael Palin*)

The Secret Diary of Adrian Mole Aged 13¾,
The Growing Pains of Adrian Mole,
The Secret Diary of Adrian Mole Song Book (*Sue Townsend*)

First published in Great Britain in 1985
by Methuen London Ltd
11 New Fetter Lane, London EC4P 4EE

ISBN 0 413 56690 0 (hardback)
       0 413 56700 1 (paperback)

Made and printed in Great Britain

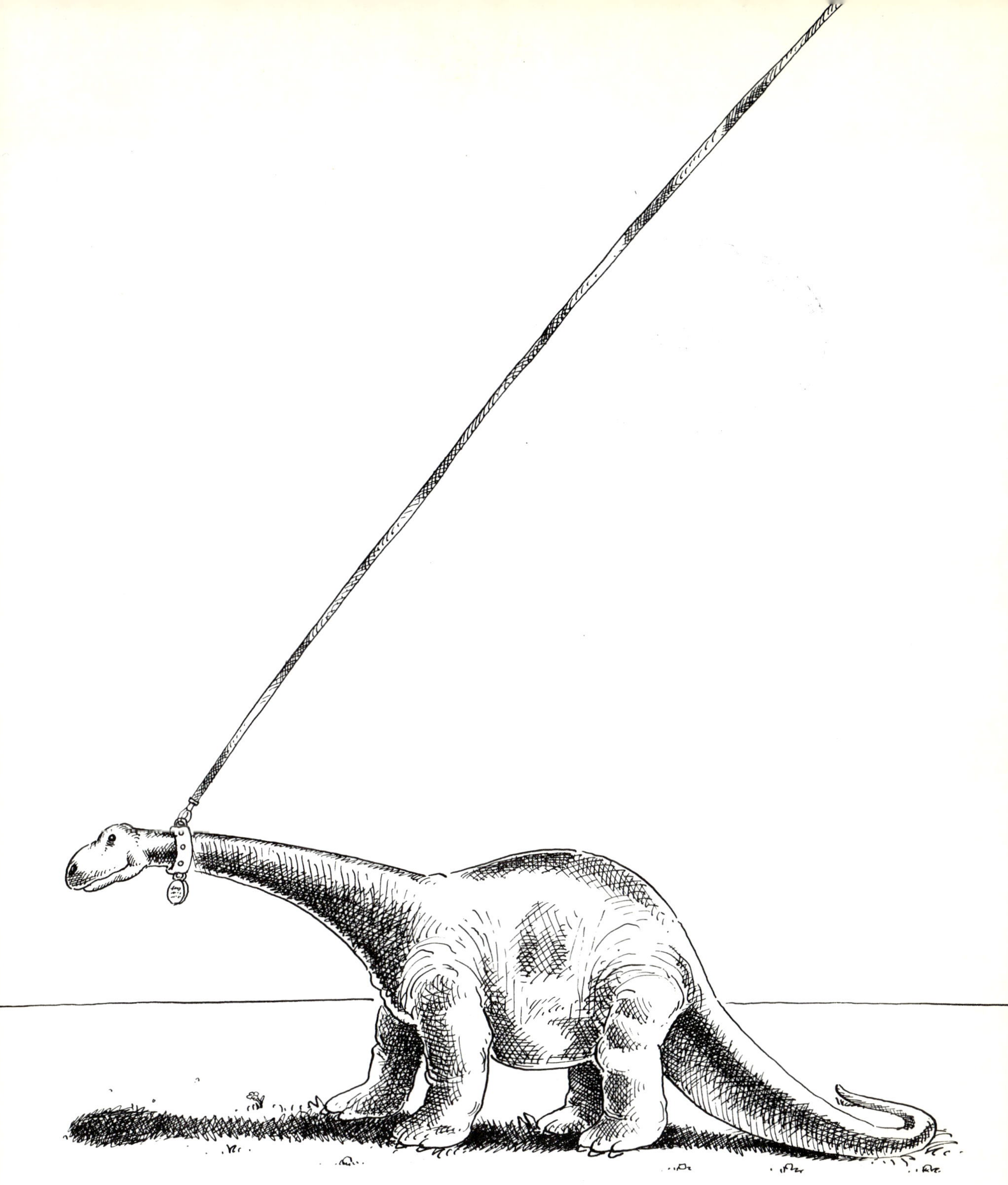

God out walking his brontosaurus

God gives a dog a bad name

76525100-60

God orders an extra pint . . .

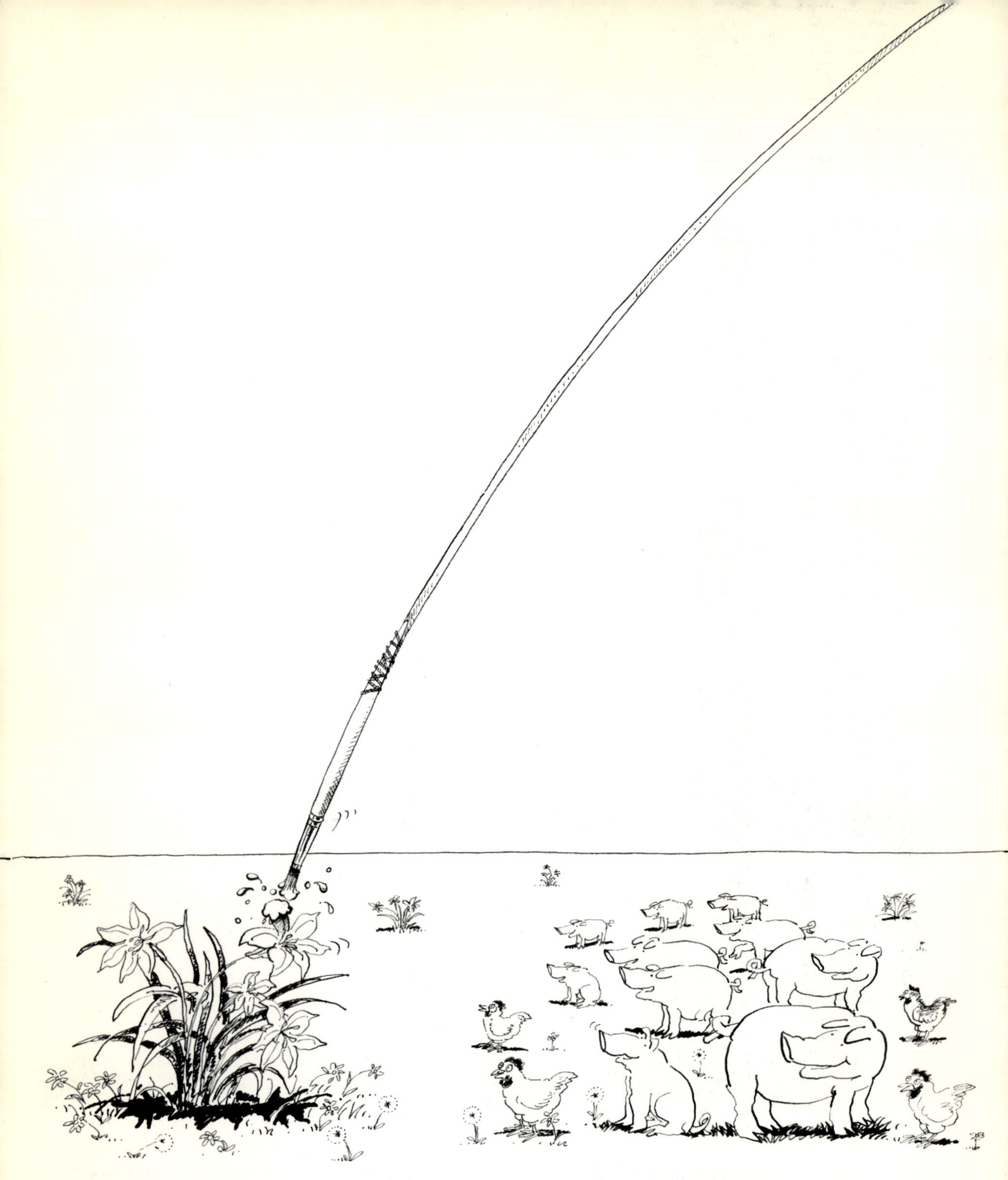

God gilds a lily

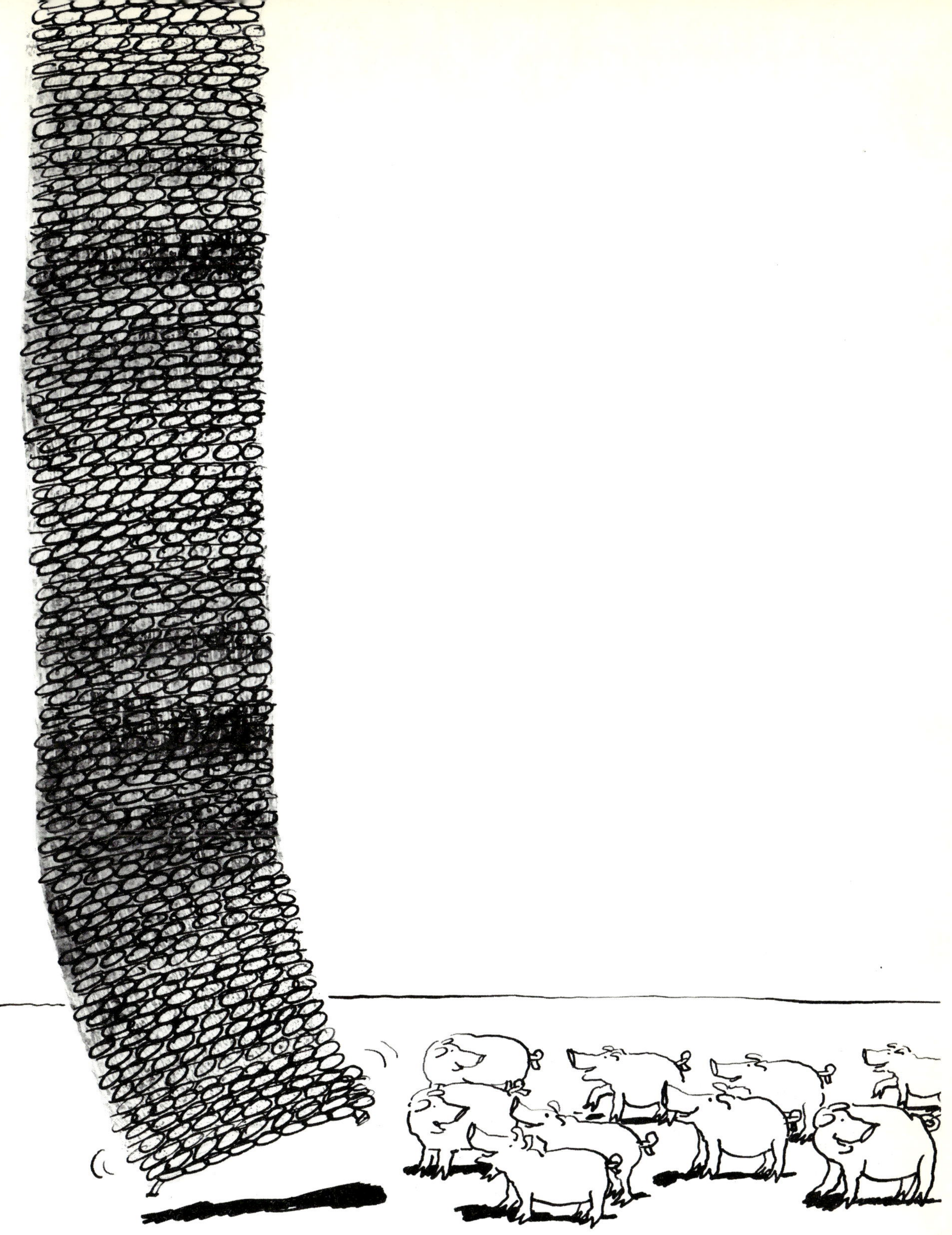

God casting purl before swine

God hanging wallpaper...

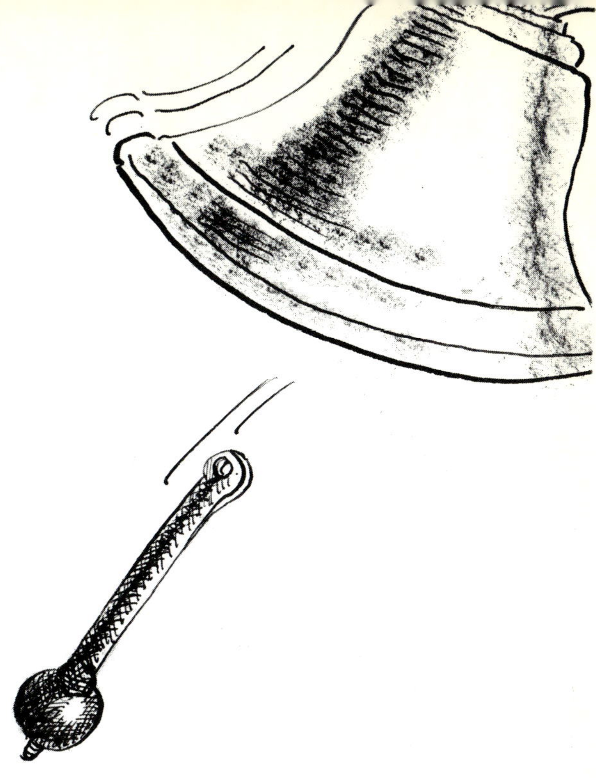

God drops a clanger

God's summer exhibition

God makes a night of it . . .

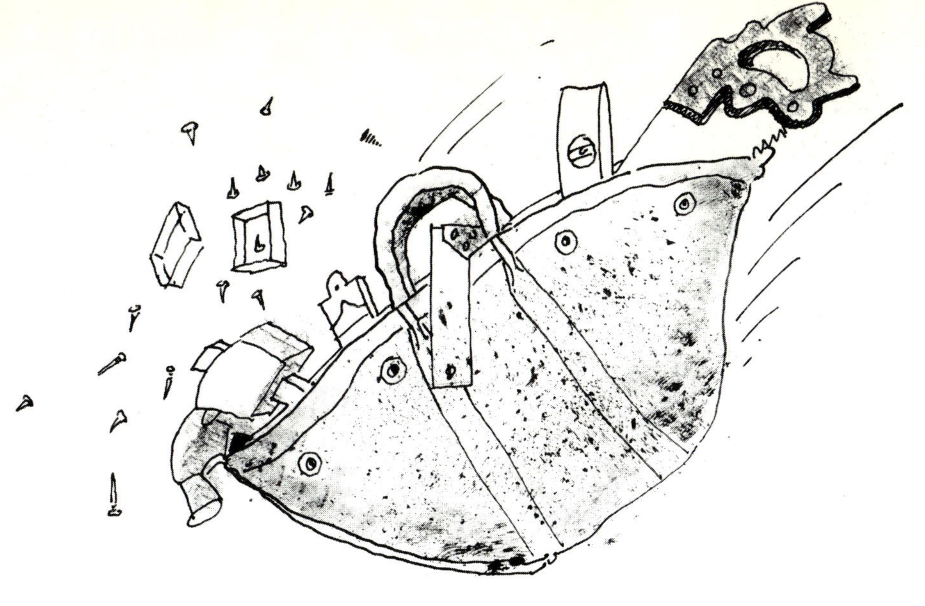

Putting up the continental shelf

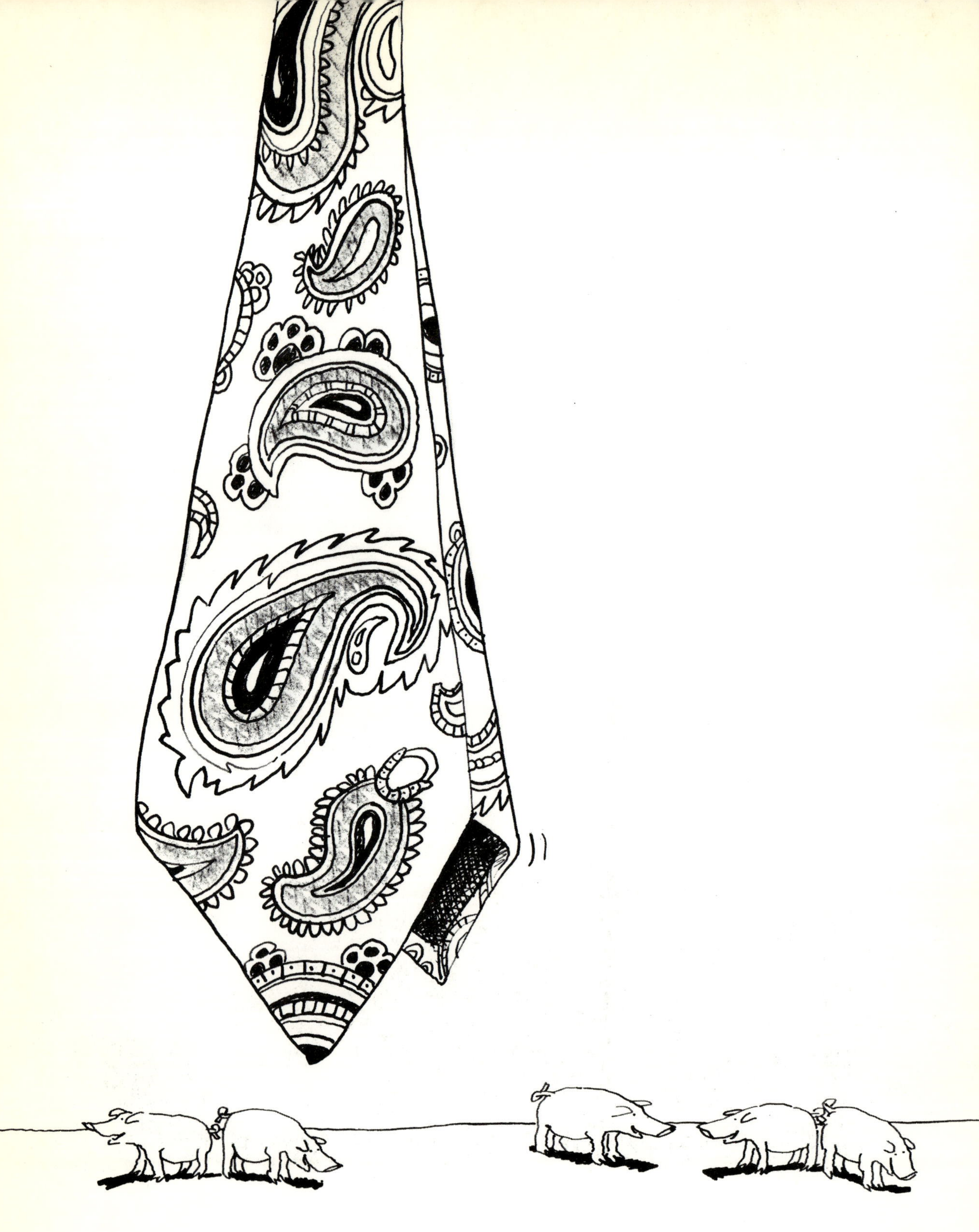

God succumbs to the dictates of fashion...

God's Hoover bites the dust

God blows his own trumpet

In order to dispel the rigours of winter
God whips up something hot

God bites off more than he can chew

God flies a kite

God drops toffees over the Atlantic,
barely missing Nova Scotia . . .

God toasts a crumpet for tea

In the beginning God created a stink . . .

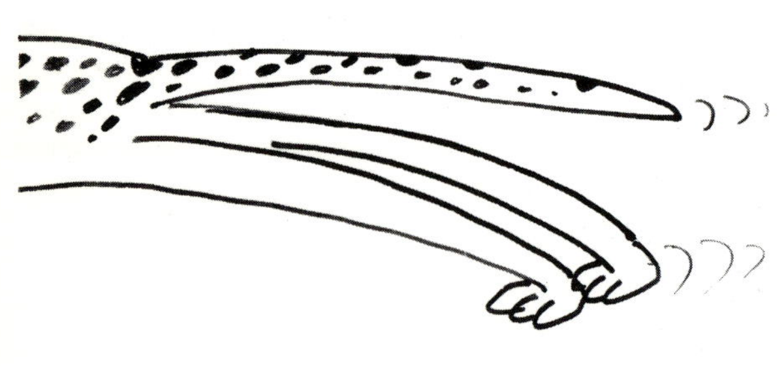

God puts the wind up a cheetah

God tempers the wind to a shorn lamb

LIMITED EDITION

Line of lassitude

DO YOU HAVE IT IN ANY OTHER COLOURS?

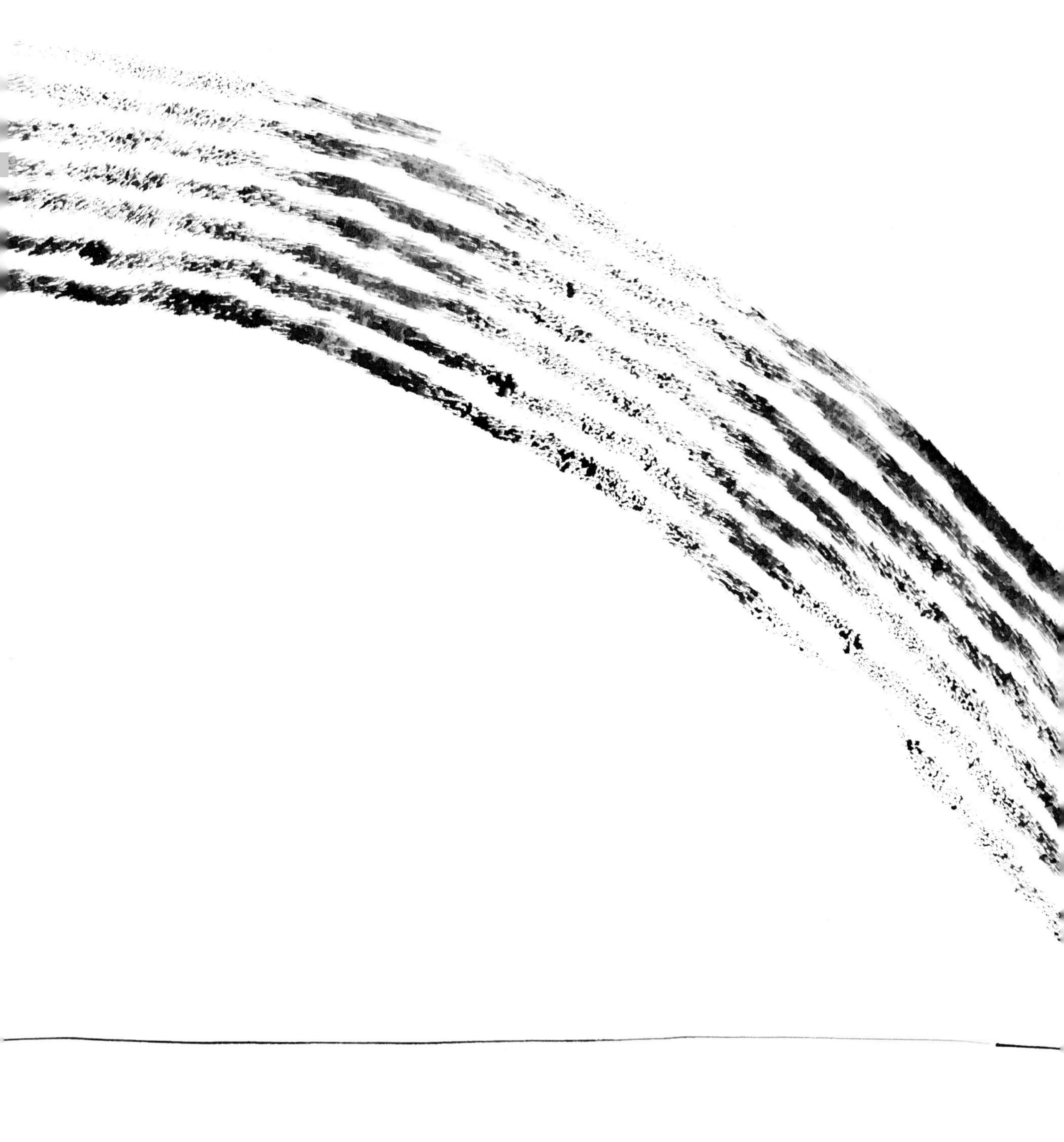

God goes too far...

Getting warm!

God spills Tippex while typing an inventory of the world so far

God gets a new fridge for Christmas

God trails clouds of Gloy

God making heavy weather of watering the lupins . . .

God throws in the trowel

God has his work cut out for him

God draws a blank

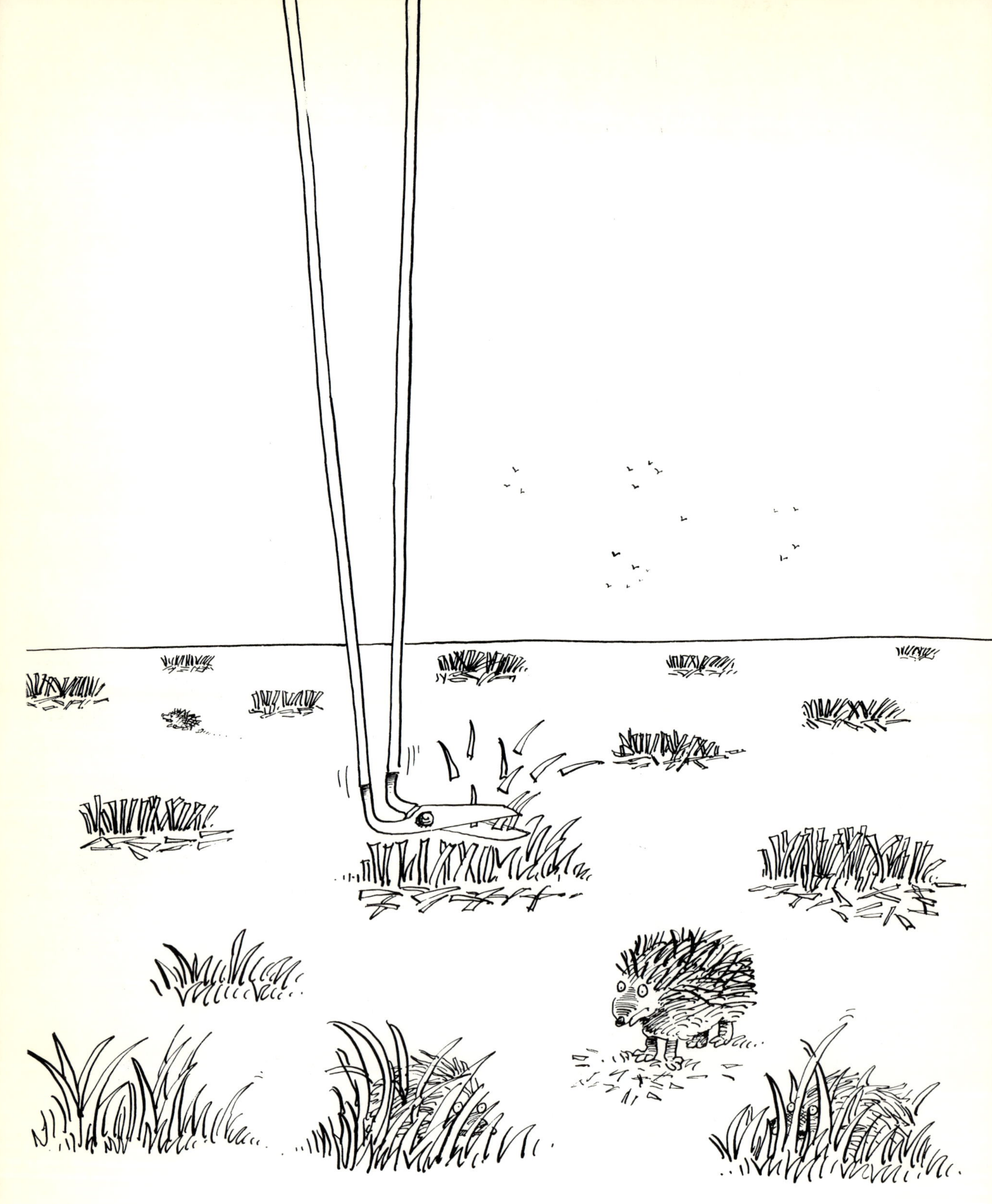

God trims tussocks at Bishop's Stortford

God knows what the cows are thinking . . .

God catches neither fish, flesh, fowl
nor good red herring...

PING.....

REJECT

Havoc caused as God coughs on Sherbet Dip-Dab...

CAUTION
WET
FLOOR

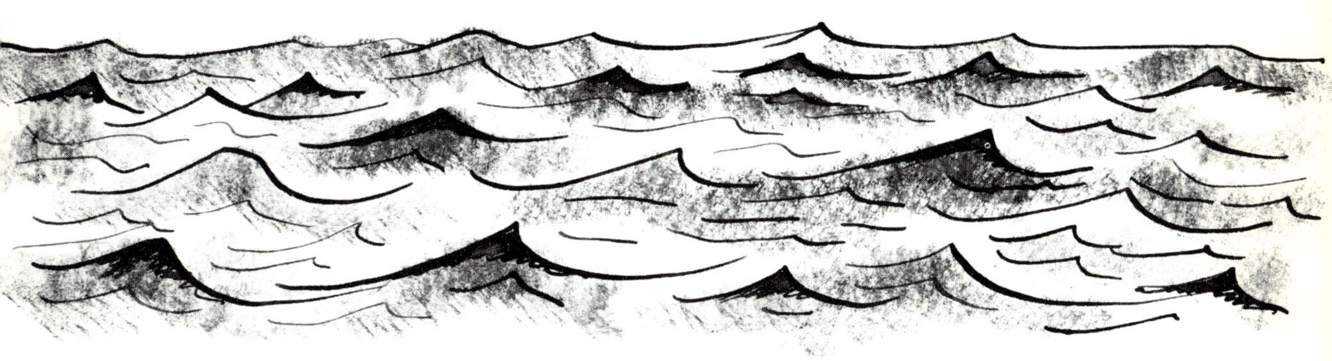

TAP
Tap
TAP
TAP
Tap

God quietens a tapping halyard

God paints the town red

God loses his marbles

Astral plane

God hedges his pets

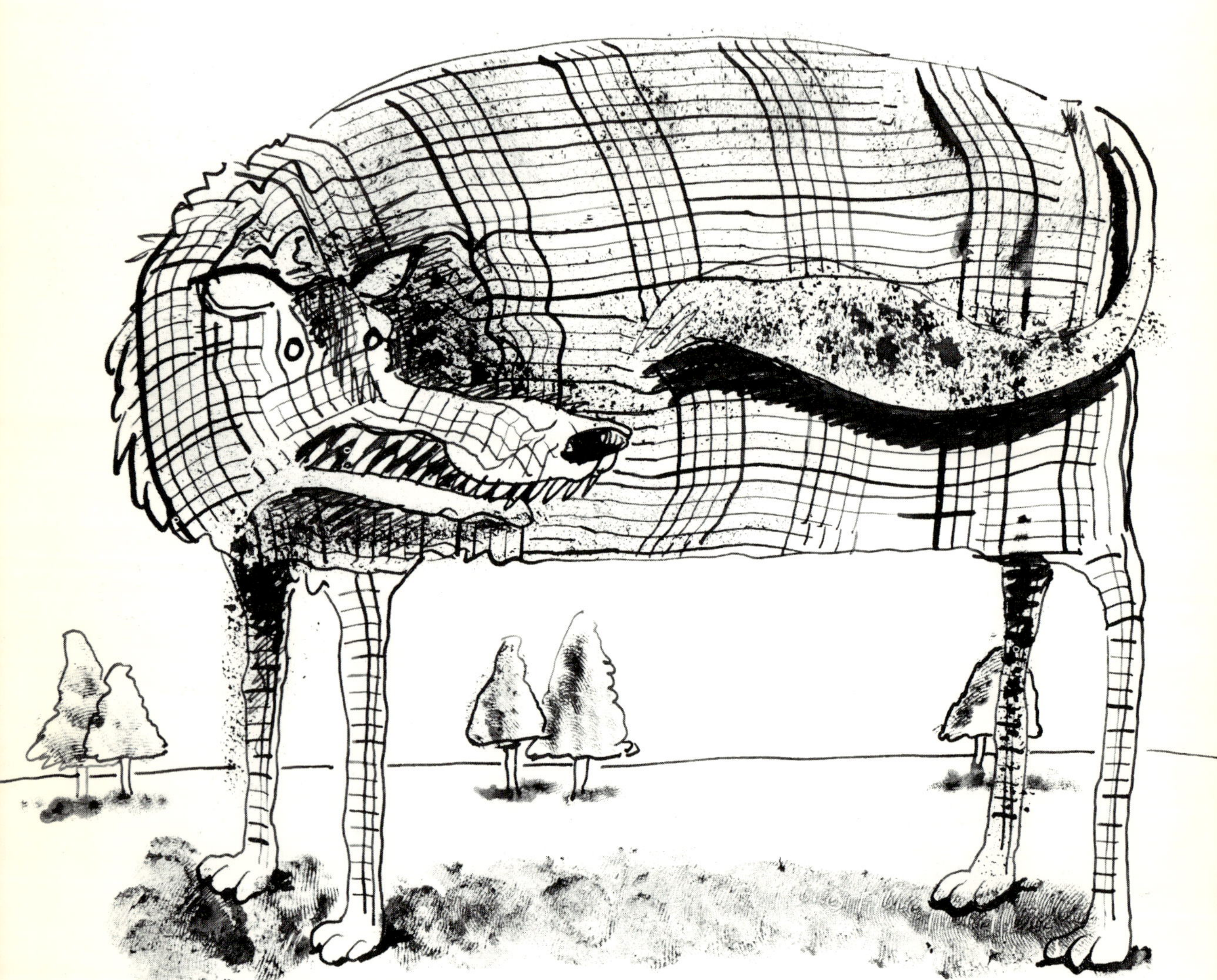

The big plaid wolf

God draws the night in . . .

God moves in a mysterious way

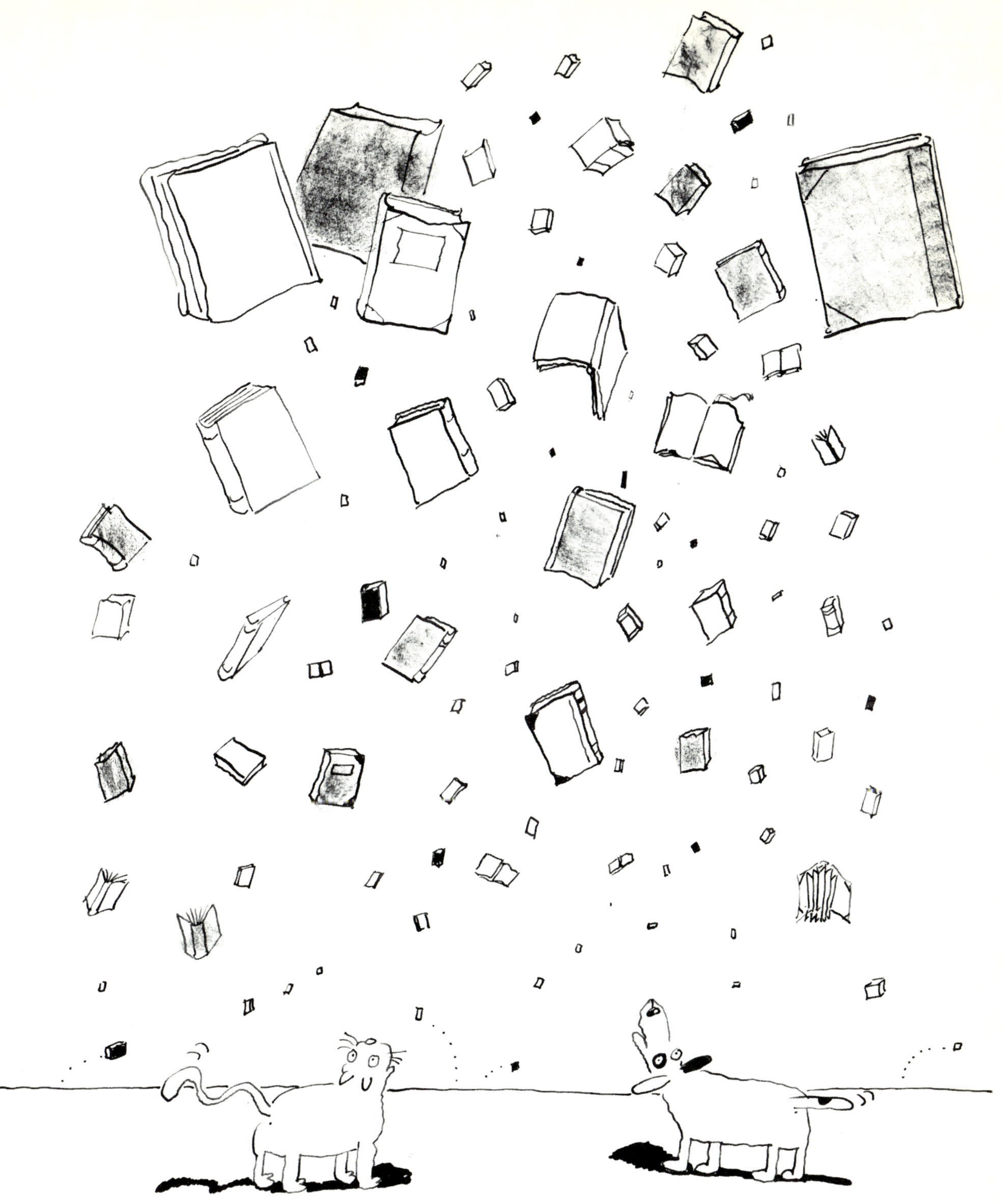

God rains catechisms and dogmas

God washes the dishes

God makes a mountain out of a molehill

God has a field day

REJECT